Scroll Saw Pictures

An Illustrated Guide to Creating Scroll Saw Art

16 New Patterns!

2nd edition

Frank Pozsgai

Text written with and photography by Douglas Congdon-Martin

Schiffer Publishing Ltd.
4880 Lower Valley Road • Atglen, PA 19310

Library of Congress Control Number: 2016960530

Cover design by Ro
Type set in Minon & Arial

ISBN: 978-0-7643-5292-8
Printed in China

Published by Schiffer Publishing, Ltd.
4880 Lower Valley Road
Atglen, PA 19310
Phone: (610) 593-1777; Fax: (610) 593-2002
E-mail: Info@schifferbooks.com
Web: www.schifferbooks.com

Contents

Introduction

This book is intended for advanced scrollers. It is meant to introduce you to the wonderful world of making scroll saw pictures.

By using various types and colors of wood as a medium, the user can create a canvas of visual delight. The process is much like *intarsia*, where an assortment of woods are used in a mosaic. It differs in that, instead of rounding over each edge, we give them a crisp sharpness. I specifically like to relieve each cut piece, then cant it to give an optimum depth of field as I insert the lighter pieces into the darker wood and vice versa. This particular art form can also be interpreted as three-dimensional cutting.

While working with various woods, I like to finish my pictures by spraying them with several coats of clear lacquer, so they look natural. However, you may want to tole paint or stain your cut-out pictures. The choice is yours.

The essential tools include a measuring tape, an assortment of blades, scissors, glue, and writing instruments.

Check to be sure the table is perfectly square before beginning.

To do this project full size we need a piece of black walnut and a piece of cherry, each 13" wide x 16" long x 1/2" thick. The dark and light color contrast is what we are after, but you could use other woods to get the same effect.

If you can't find wood of the dimension you want, you will need to joint the narrower pieces together with glue.

5

Select a pattern. This is called "Wolf Pack," and is designed by Sue Chaffee, who has a tee shirt company in Portland, Oregon. She kindly gave us permission to use this pattern.

6

I have decided to use a portion of the picture, and have enlarged it to fit on my wood.

7

While it may not seem to make any difference, it is helpful to have the lighter wood on the bottom. When you insert your blade through a drilled hole, the lighter wood makes it easier to see. Align the wood and tape it together at the corners with masking tape.

8

Use a generous amount to keep it secure during the process of cutting. You don't want the wood to shift while you are working on it.

9

Center the pattern where you want it.

10

There is a lot of detail in this pattern so we need to apply an even coat of glue across the whole thing to ensure that it is well-adhered. I use a common GlueStick™ for this.

11

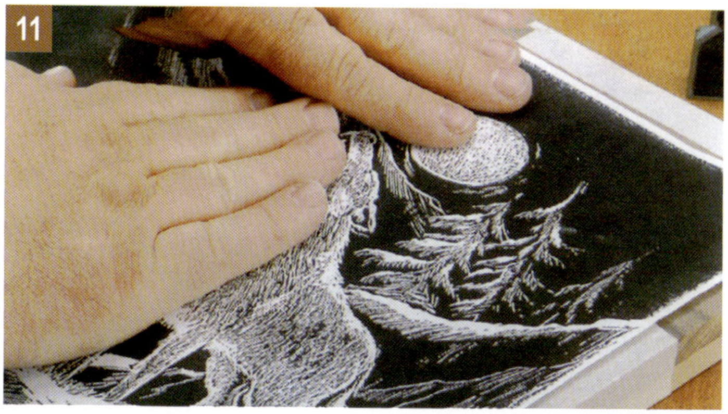

Working from the center, smooth out the paper pattern so there are no air bubbles.

12

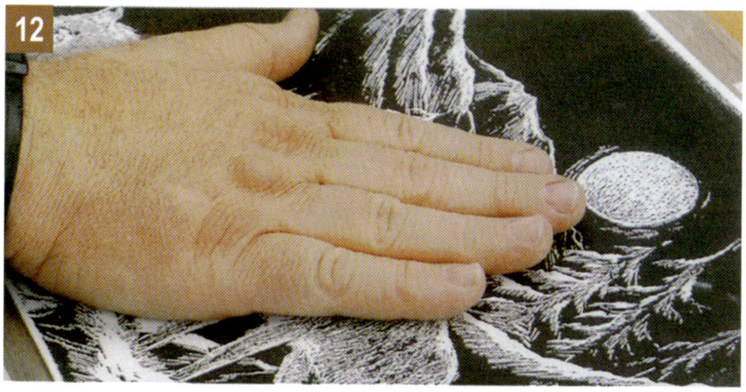

Follow this with a circular wiping motion.

13

Look at the pattern for places to drill your holes. Wherever possible you want the holes to be at a place where the wood turns, so they will be camouflaged. This point between the legs is a good example of such a spot.

14

You will not want to use every line of a pattern. You must choose the areas that you will cut and outline them.

15

You want to create enough lines and spaces to define the figure you are cutting, but not so many that the details overpower the work. Here I've outlined the eyes and set the general shape of the snout and jaw.

16

Where the pattern ends, continue the lines into the wood in an "aesthetically" pleasing way, rather than harshly cropping the ends.

17

Before you drill the first hole you want to have a plan. You need to determine what the main areas of the work are and where the lines will go. Spend enough time drawing and checking to make sure you have it right.

Drill the pattern using a 1/16" bit. If at all possible use a drill press, or a press jig for your hand drill to be certain the holes are perpendicular. Because we are going to mix the woods from the two pieces, the holes and cuts must be identical. Whenever possible begin in a corner; this camouflages the hole.

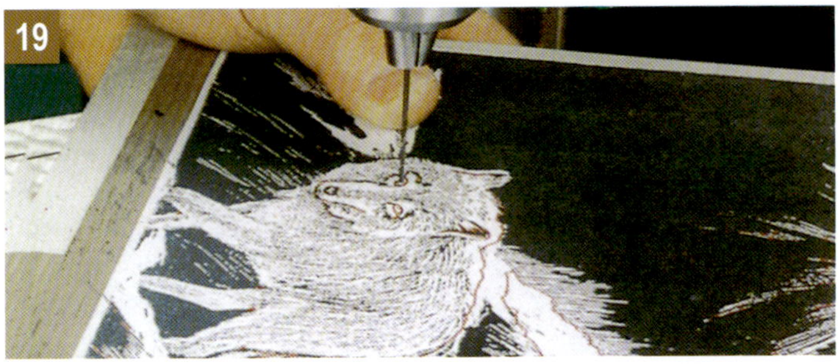

The eyes and nose of this wolf are going to be cut away completely, so you can drill right through the center.

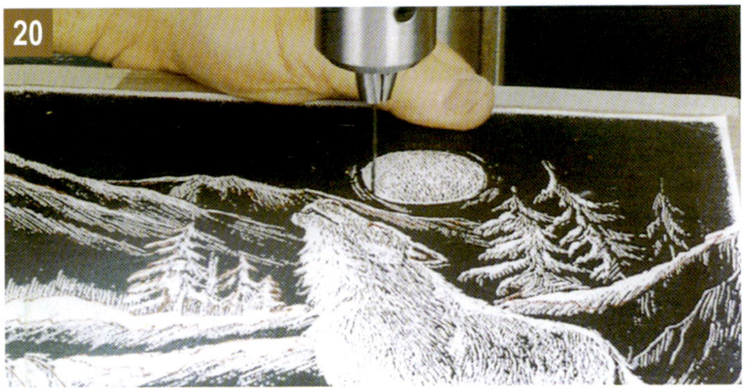

The full moon has no corners, so we must drill right on the edge.

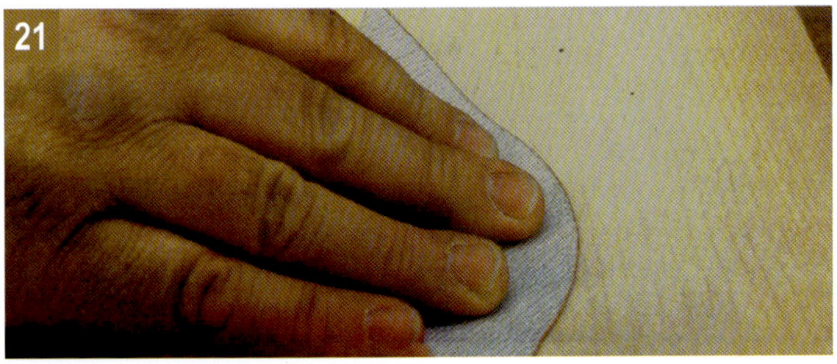

Lightly sand the underside with 320 paper to take away the burrs from drilling. This will make it easier to see holes when inserting the saw blades. It also helps the wood glide more smoothly across the surface of the table.

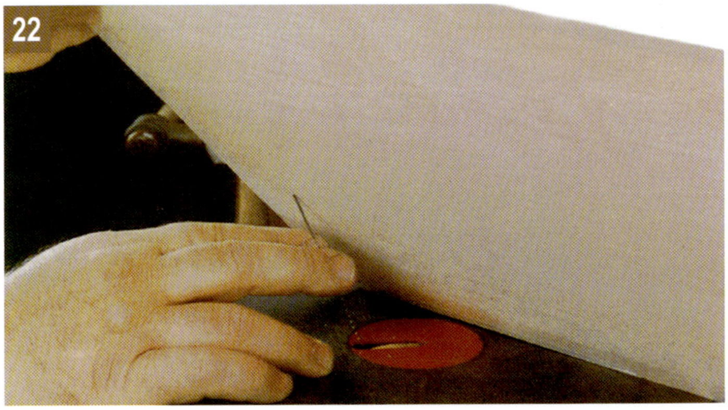

I use a #9 PGT (Precision Ground Tooth) blade for this project, though you could use a #7. You can start sawing anywhere. I'll start with the mountains and work down through the picture. Insert the blade from beneath.

Feed the piece at the speed the saw dictates. Keep the feed even and don't force it. You want the blade to stay as straight as possible through the cut to keep the two pieces identical.

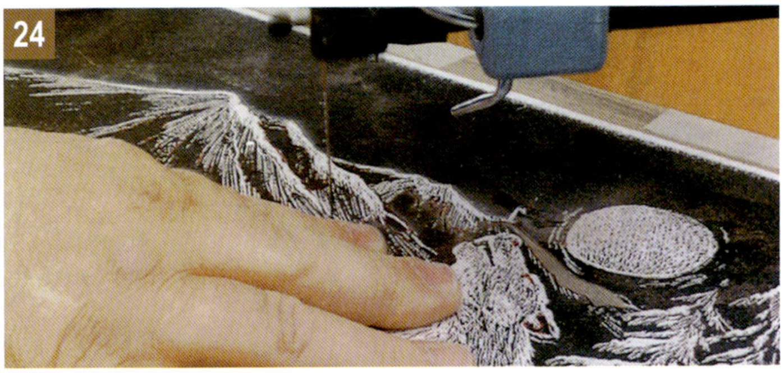

On a large piece like this, one hand stays close to the blade. This steadies the work, keeps it on the table, and controls the wood. The other hand makes the pivots and feeds the wood.

When creating a picture like this, you don't need to worry too much about staying on the lines. The picture is in the contrast between the positive and negative spaces, and you can vary the cut without harming the effect.

26

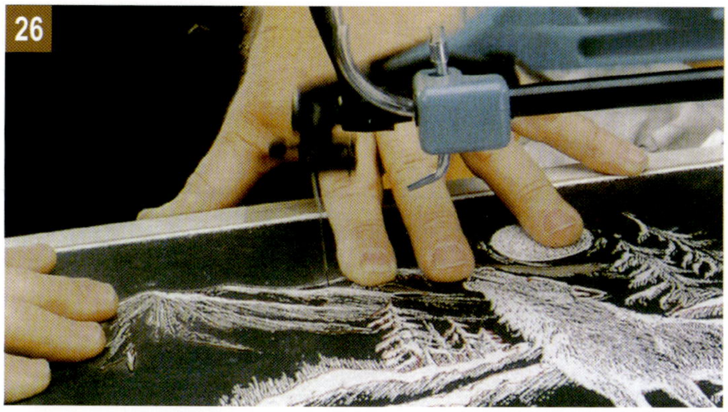

Remove the blade and reinsert it to do the inside cuts in the mountain range. You will probably find it easier to do all the inside cuts first.

27

Remove the cut out pieces as you go, and put them aside for future use.

28

The blade will be abused during the changes in this project and will probably get bent beyond use. Check it and change it as necessary.

29

Continue with the moon...

30

and the forest areas.

31

Coming back between the trees you need to be careful not to cut over something you have cut before.

32

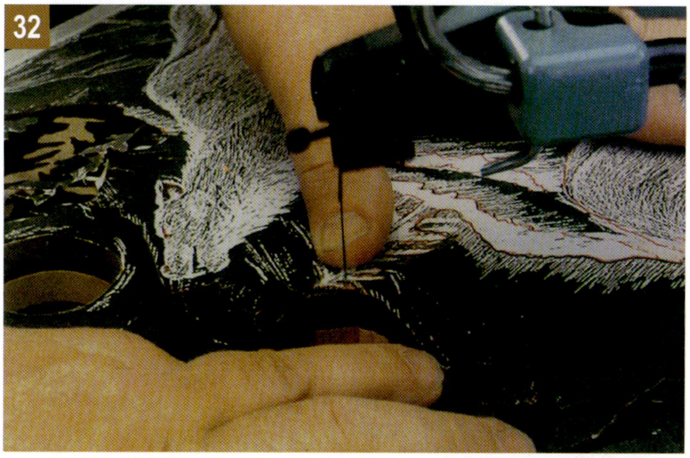

When some things have been removed, be careful not to put pressure on some weak point and break it off.

By pulling the paper away from the more fragile areas, you can keep a better eye on them.

Be careful, too, during blade changes.

The wolves and ground where they sit are all one piece. Begin work on them by doing the inside cuts first. I start with the ear.

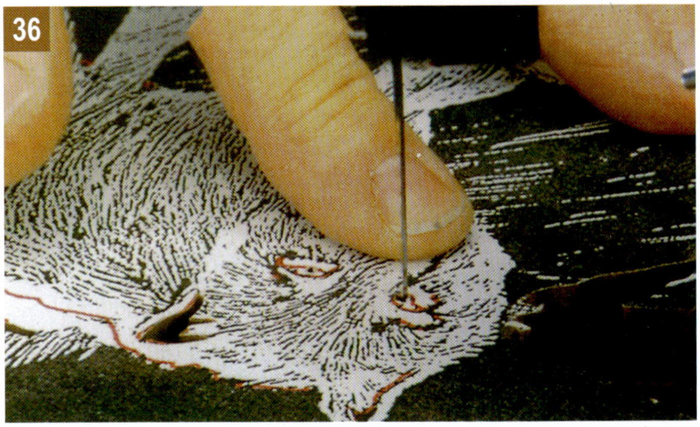

The eye will be cut out completely.

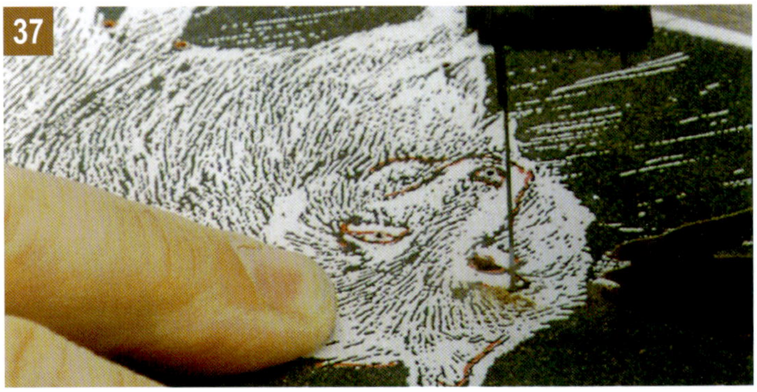

Go from the corner and make lines that define the forehead ...

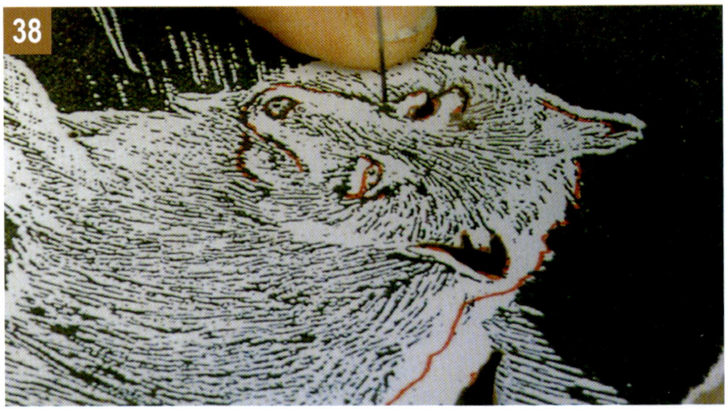

and the snout and neck.

Cut out the nose. Again, this will be an empty spot.

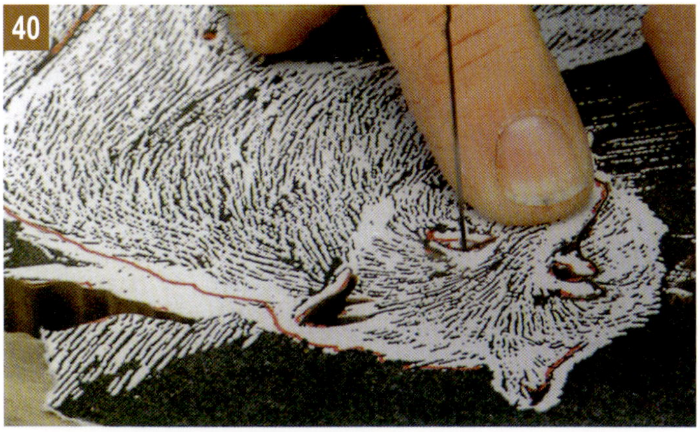

Continue with the other eye and the lines of the head.

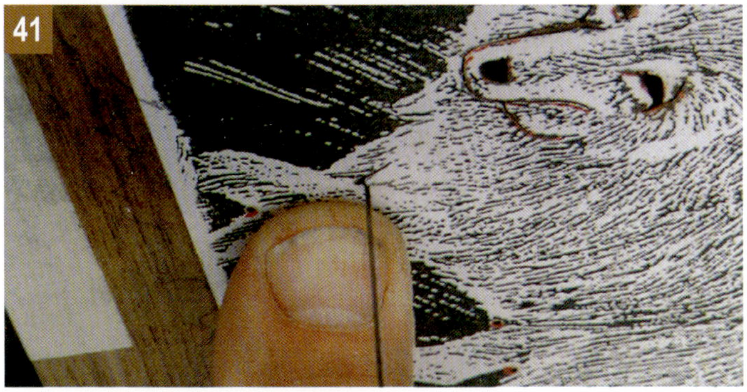

A simple V defines the chest.

With the details done, cut the open areas.

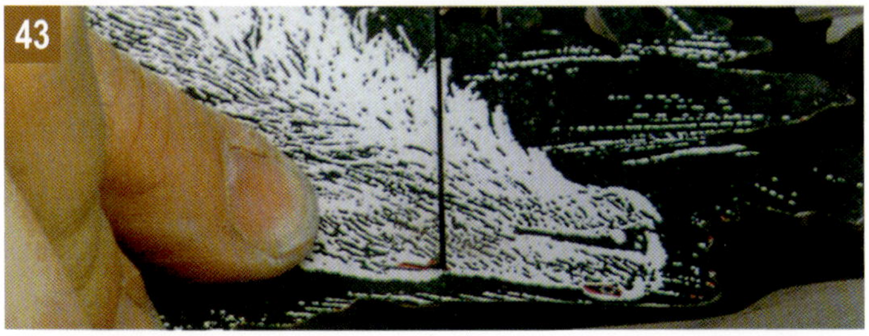

Move to the baying wolf's eye. Start in the corner. By moving the work around the blade you get the effect of rasping the eye out.

Cut the nose...

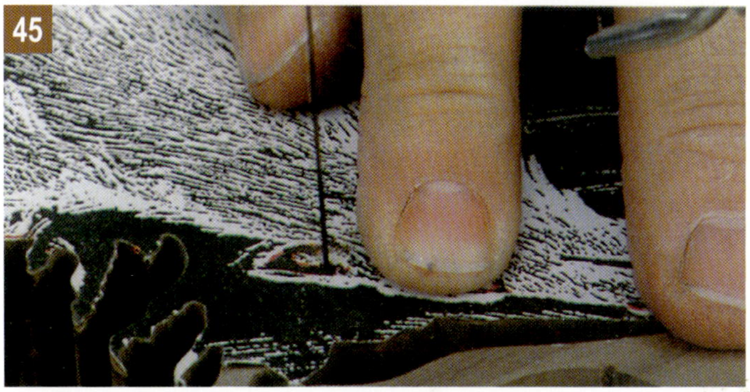

and the ear and you are ready for the outline.

Cut the outline of the wolves.

Around the hair you want to add some details by pivoting the board...

as you cut.

Where your pattern runs out you will have to improvise. You may draw these lines first or do it freehand as I have.

You will make a more interesting piece if you don't make these background lines too straight.

Particular care will be needed around the nose and in the mouth, to keep the details intact.

Keep as much of the hair detail as you can.

Remove larger pieces of paper from the board ...

and the cut-outs. Don't sand until the pieces are reassembled. There are delicate nooks and crannies that could break if sanded now.

Reassemble the pieces, light in light and dark in dark.

Ready for sanding.

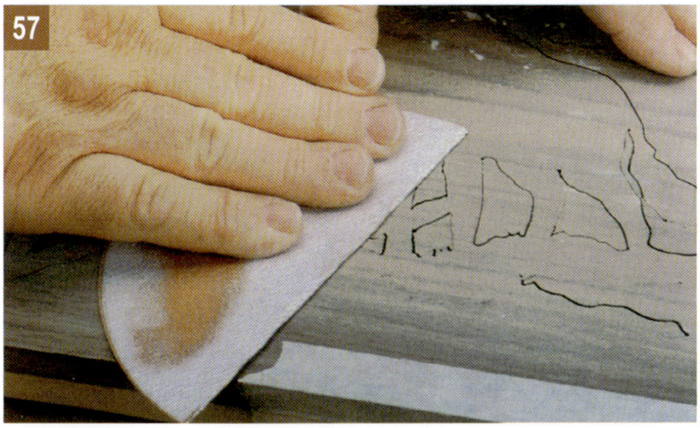

Hand sand, using 320 grit paper while pushing down on the pieces to keep them flush. Make sure all the glue is removed or it will show through the finish. Machine sanding is too aggressive for this work and would probably break some of the finer points.

Remove the tape and separate the pieces. If there is any residue from the tape, lightly sand it with 320 grit paper.

Lightly sand the other surface.

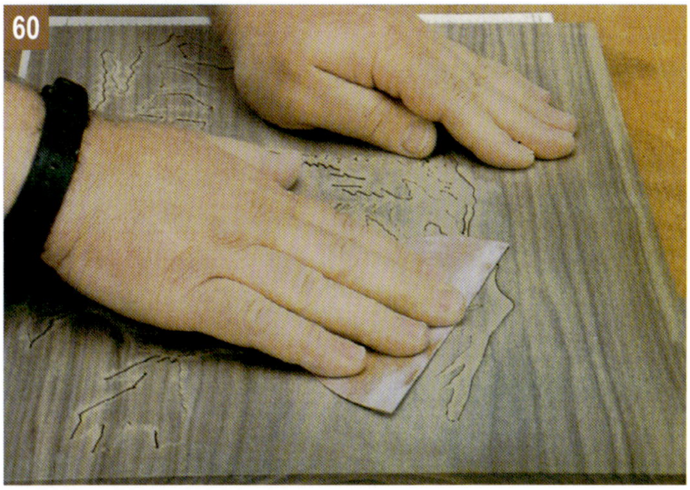

Finally, sand the back sides of the wood.

61

Place the light wood in the dark. It can be flush...

62

or canted out for a more three-dimensional effect.

63

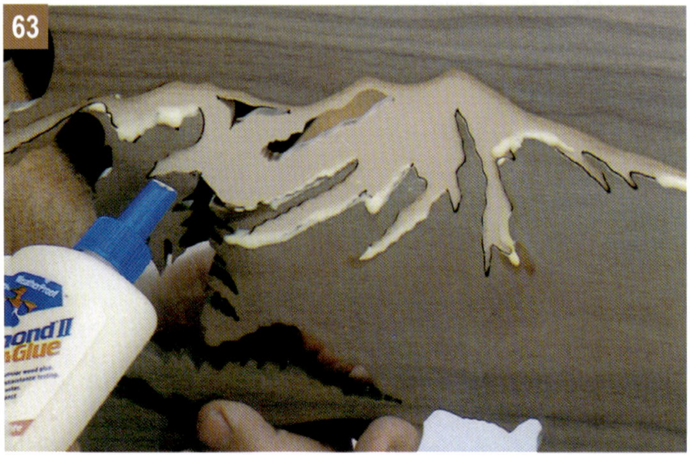

When you are satisfied, tack it in place with glue from the back.

64

Wipe away the excess with your finger. (The back of this piece will never be seen, which lets you get away with a lot.)

65

Before the glue dries you have time to make final adjustments. Here I have the right end of the mountains (light wood) flush with the darker wood and the left end protruding out from the surface.

66

Do the same thing with the dark wood in the light background.

Install the dark cut-outs in the light mountains.

The moon is flush with the surface and turned just slightly to help conceal the drill hole.

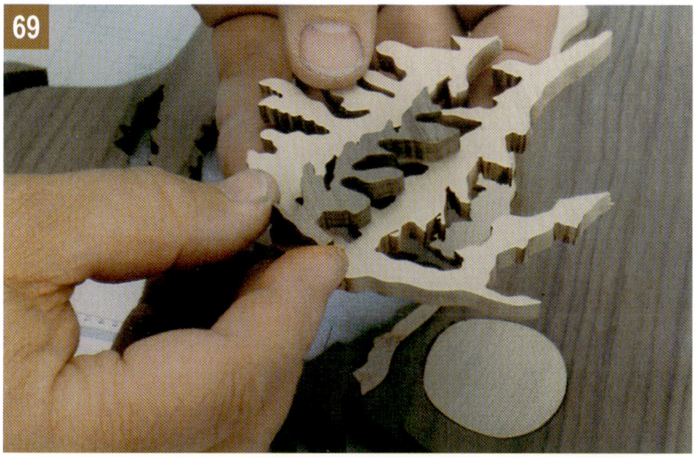

This fragile part from between the trees broke out while sawing. Now is the time to fix it as we glue the trees in place.

While the trees can come out from the background, the middle section should be flush.

Glue the wolves into place before adding the cut-outs.

When I've set the angle I want, I use my thumb to hold it in position while gluing.

The cut-outs of the wolves should be flush with the background surface.

One finished!

With a table saw, rip walnut and cherry into strips 1/2" x 1/4". These will be cut to lengths to frame the pictures. In this case, we have two pieces each 16" long and two pieces each that are 11 15/16". These are glued in place around the edge.

Spray with a clear finish and its ready for hanging or for placing in that special niche.

The Gallery

Brandy

SCHUTZEN

This pattern was created by Susan Chaffee, of Vancouver, Washington. She is a renowned wildlife artist and the owner of Sue Chaffee Originals, at the Lloyd Center in Portland, Oregon. This drawing in entitled "Wolf Pack" and is used with permission.

Patterns

I recommend that you enlarge the pattern 185%. The wood thickness can be 1/8", 1/4", or 1/2".

I recommend you enlarge the patterns on this page 200%.
The wood thickness can be 1/8", 1/4", or 1/2".

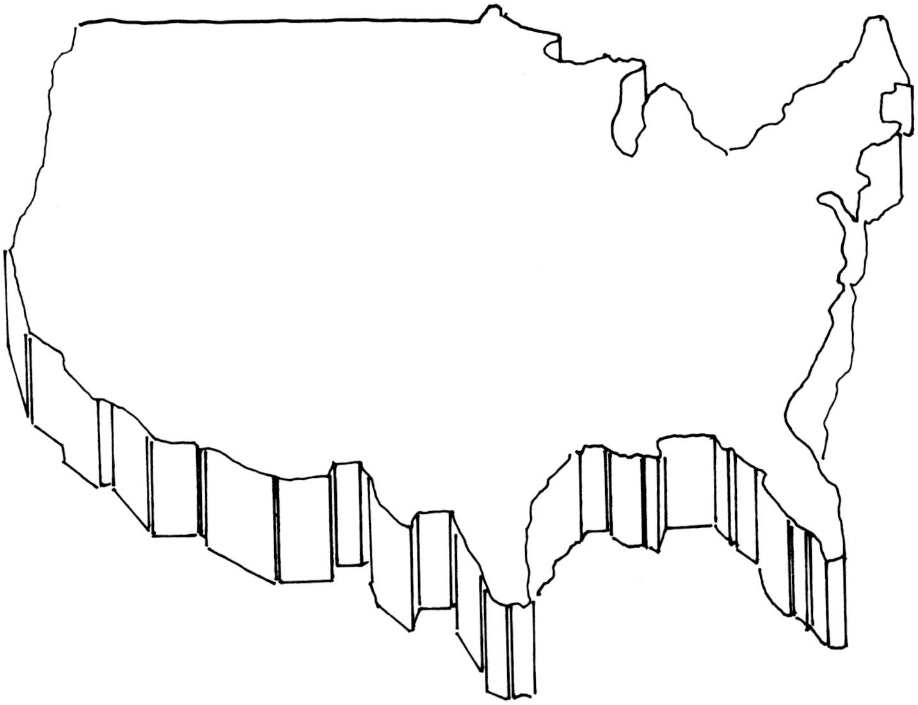

I recommend you enlarge the patterns on this page 200%.
The wood thickness can be 1/8", 1/4", or 1/2".

I recommend you enlarge the patterns on this page 200%. The wood thickness can be 1/8", 1/4", or 1/2".

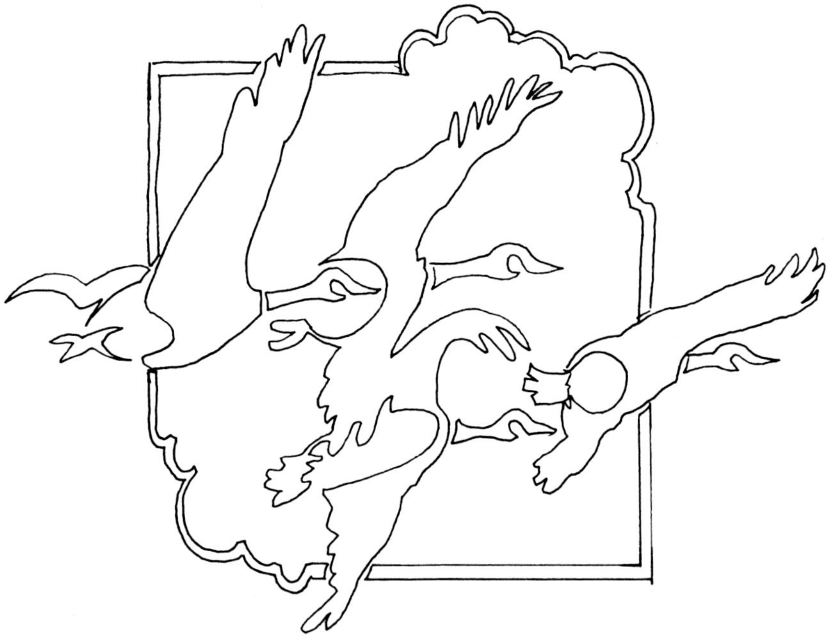

I recommend you enlarge the patterns on this page 200%.
The wood thickness can be 1/8", 1/4", or 1/2".

I recommend you enlarge the patterns on this page 200%. The wood thickness can be 1/8", 1/4", or 1/2".

I recommend you enlarge the patterns on this page 200%. The wood thickness can be 1/8", 1/4", or 1/2".

I recommend you enlarge the patterns on this page 200%. The wood thickness can be 1/8", 1/4", or 1/2".

I recommend you enlarge the patterns on this page 200%. The wood thickness can be 1/8", 1/4", or 1/2".

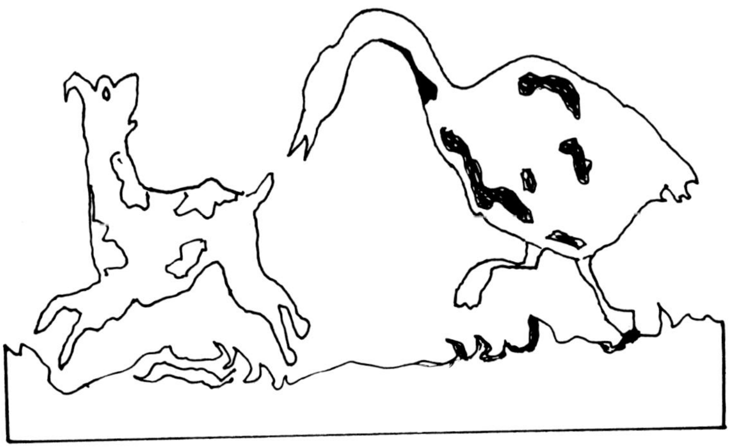

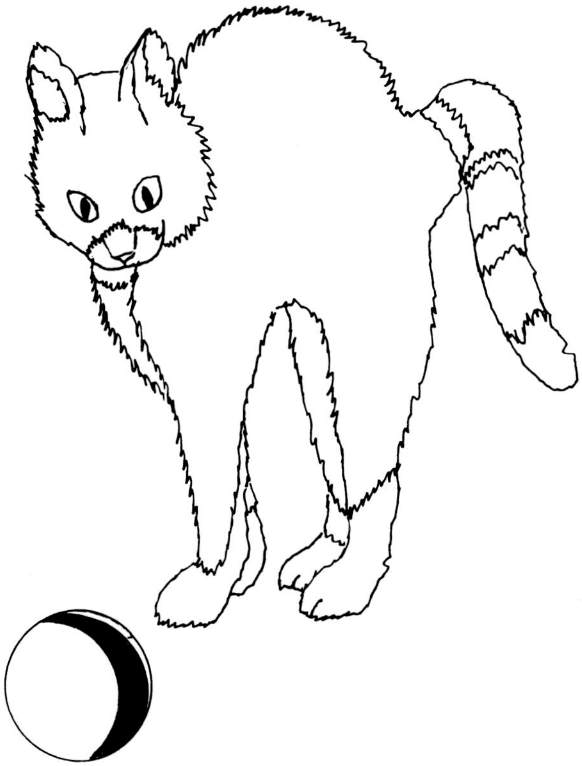

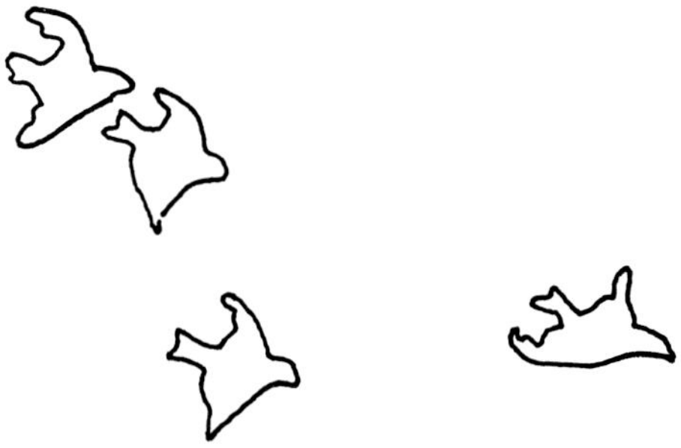

I recommend you enlarge the patterns on this page 200%. The wood thickness can be 1/8", 1/4", or 1/2".

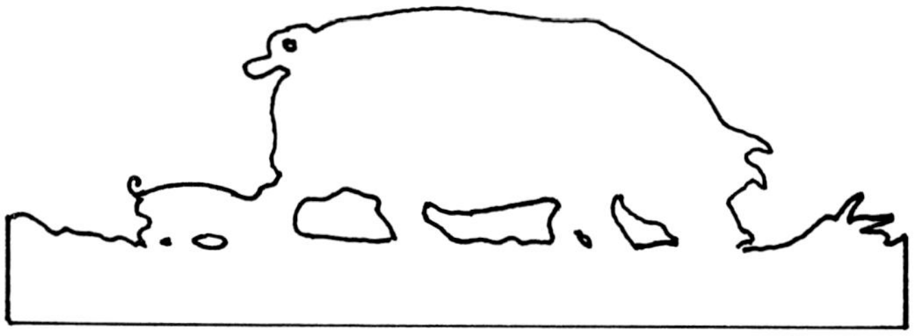

I recommend you enlarge the patterns on this page 200%. The wood thickness can be 1/8", 1/4", or 1/2".

I recommend you enlarge the patterns on this page 200%. The wood thickness can be 1/8", 1/4", or 1/2".

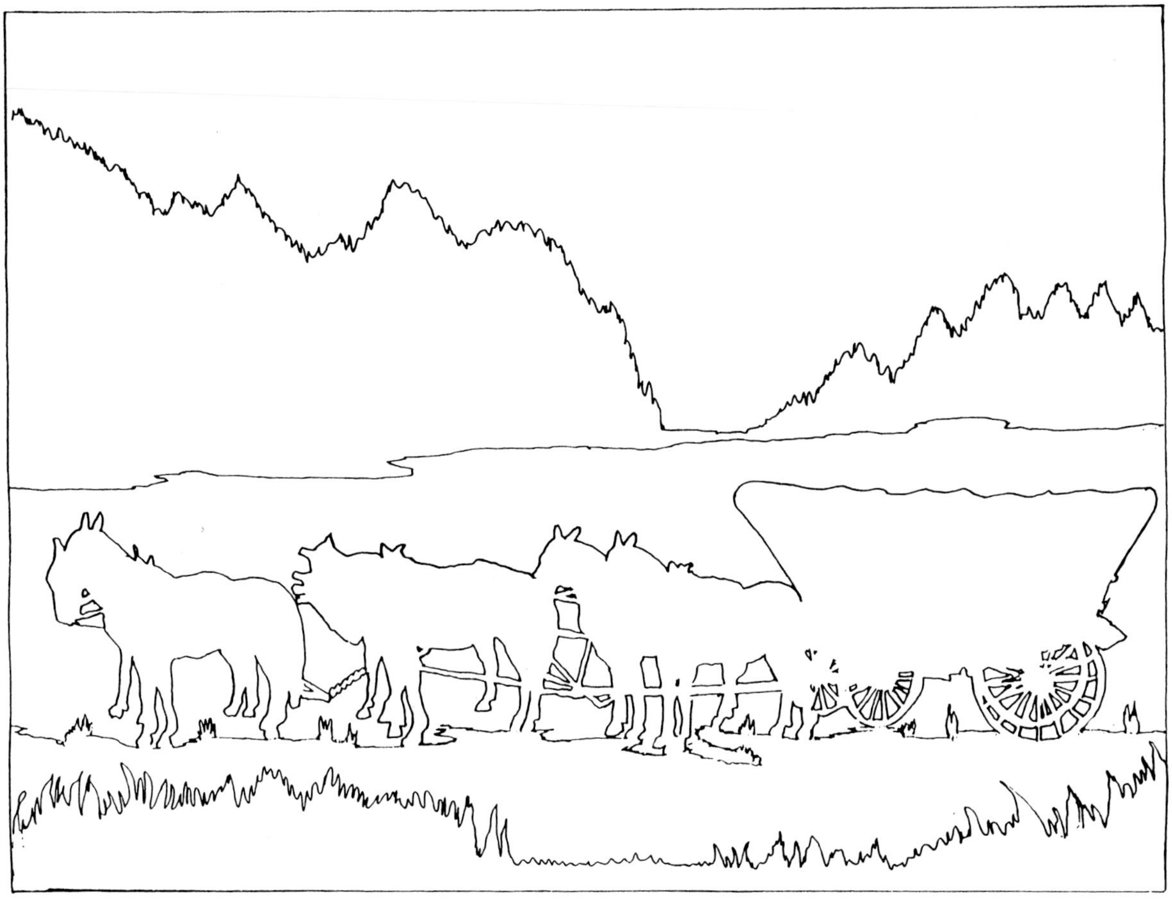

I recommend you enlarge this pattern 250%.
The wood thickness can be 1/8", 1/4", or 1/2".

I recommend you enlarge this pattern 250%.
The wood thickness can be 1/8", 1/4", or 1/2".

I recommend you enlarge this pattern 200%. The wood thickness can be 1/8", 1/4", or 1/2".

I recommend you enlarge the patterns on this page 200%.
The wood thickness can be 1/8", 1/4", or 1/2".

I recommend you enlarge the patterns on this page 200%. The wood thickness can be 1/8", 1/4", or 1/2".

I recommend you enlarge the patterns on this page 200%. The wood thickness can be 1/8", 1/4", or 1/2".

I recommend you enlarge the patterns on this page 200%. The wood thickness can be 1/8", 1/4", or 1/2".

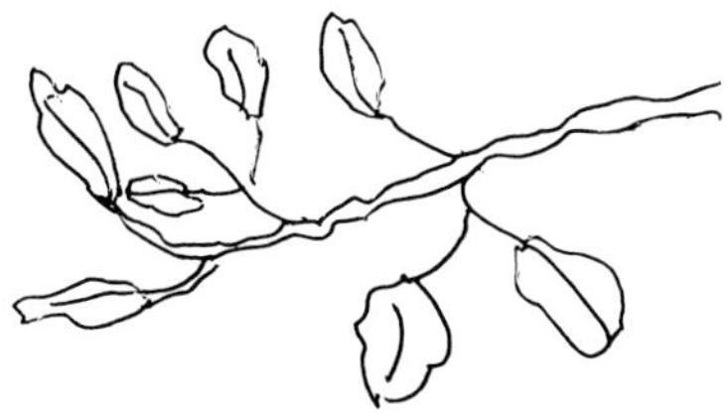

I recommend you enlarge the patterns on this page 200%. The wood thickness can be 1/8", 1/4", or 1/2".

I recommend you enlarge the patterns on this page 200%. The wood thickness can be 1/8", 1/4", or 1/2".

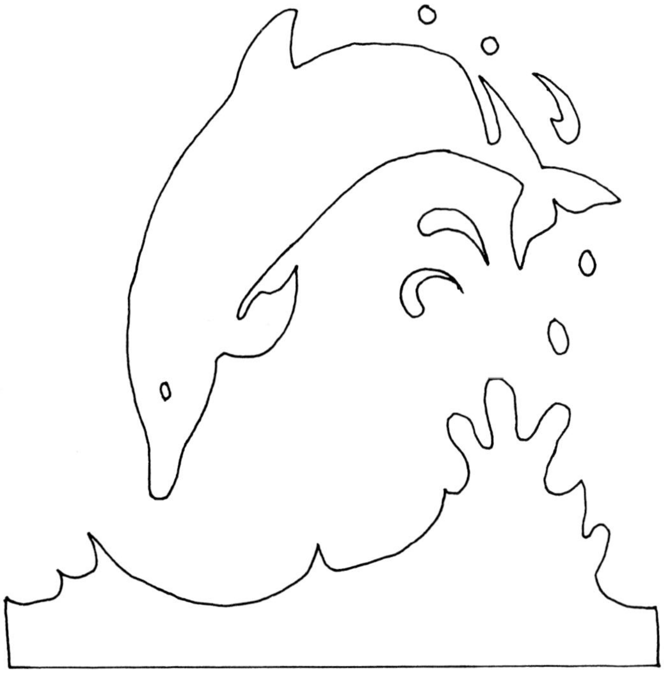

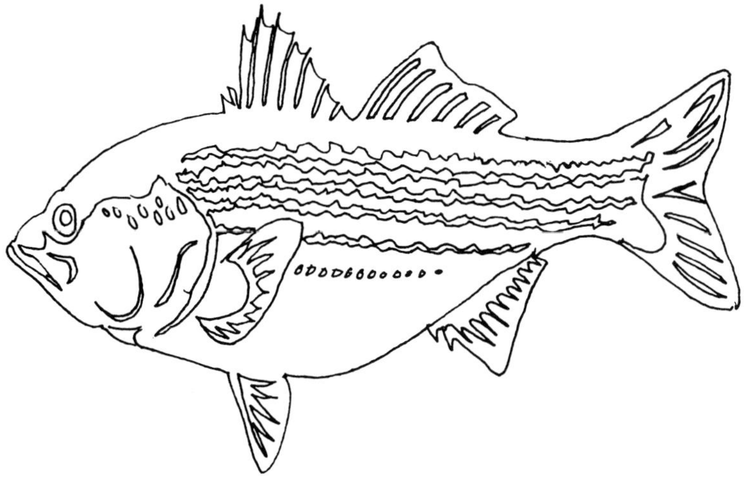

I recommend you enlarge the patterns on this page 200%.
The wood thickness can be 1/8", 1/4", or 1/2".

I recommend you enlarge the patterns on this page 200%. The wood thickness can be 1/8", 1/4", or 1/2".

I recommend you enlarge the patterns on this page 200%. The wood thickness can be 1/8", 1/4", or 1/2".

I recommend you enlarge the patterns on this page 200%. The wood thickness can be 1/8", 1/4", or 1/2".

I recommend you enlarge the patterns on this page 200%. The wood thickness can be 1/8", 1/4", or 1/2".

I recommend you enlarge the patterns 130%. The wood thickness can be 1/8", 1/4", or 1/2".

I recommend you enlarge this patterns 130%. The wood thickness can be 1/8", 1/4", or 1/2".

I recommend you enlarge the patterns on this page 200%. The wood thickness can be 1/8", 1/4", or 1/2".

I recommend you enlarge the patterns on this page 200%. The wood thickness can be 1/8", 1/4", or 1/2".

I recommend you enlarge the patterns on this page 200%. The wood thickness can be 1/8", 1/4", or 1/2".

I recommend you enlarge the patterns on this page 200%. The wood thickness can be 1/8", 1/4", or 1/2".

I recommend you use this pattern at full size. The wood thickness can be 1/8", 1/4", or 1/2".

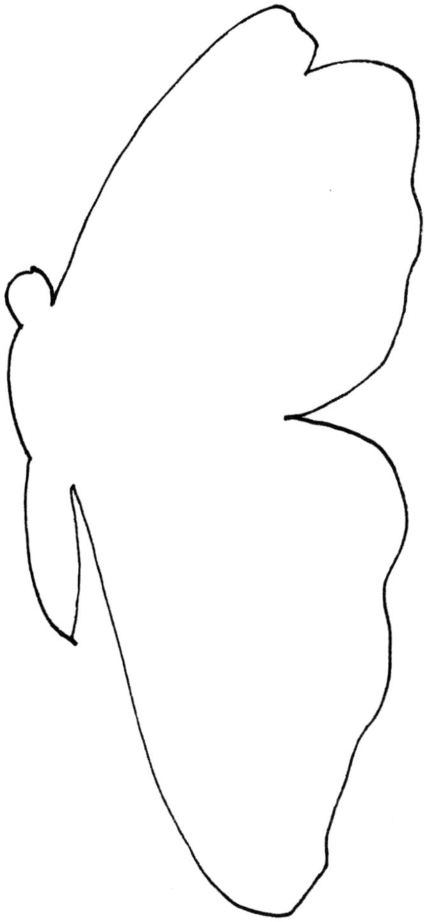

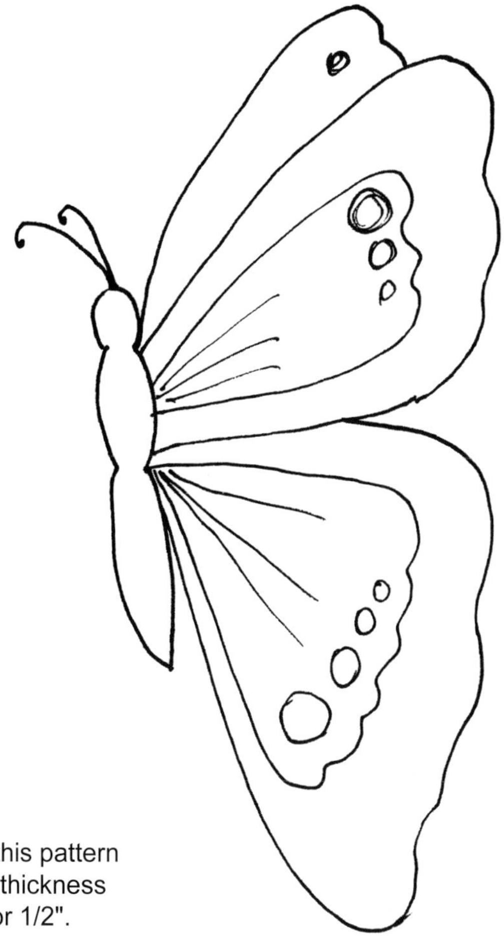

I recommend you use this pattern at full size. The wood thickness can be 1/8", 1/4", or 1/2".

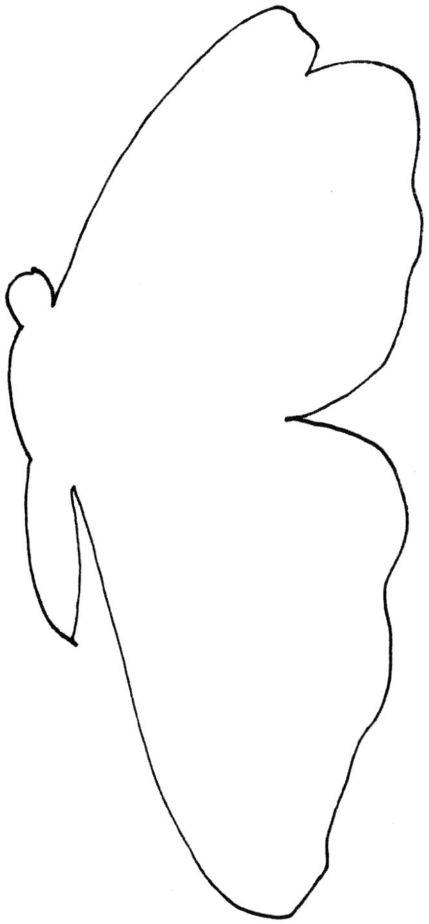

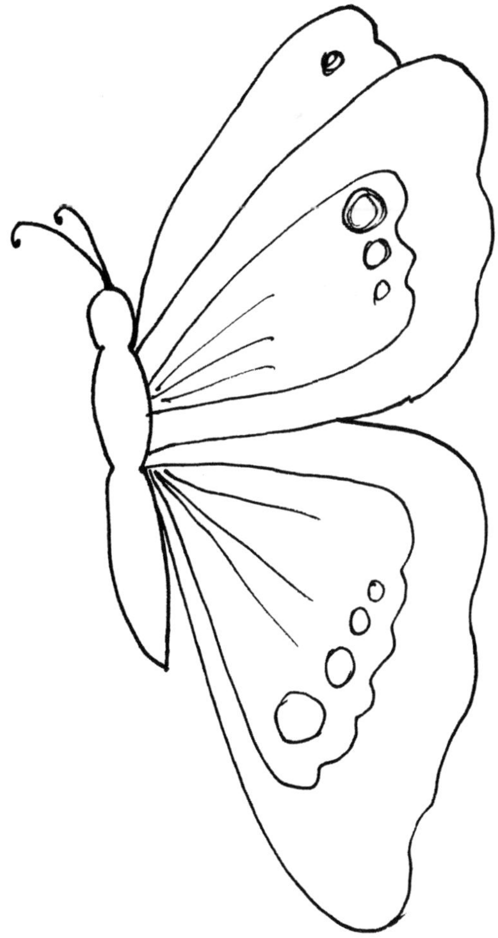

I recommend you use this pattern at full size. The wood thickness can be 1/8", 1/4", or 1/2".

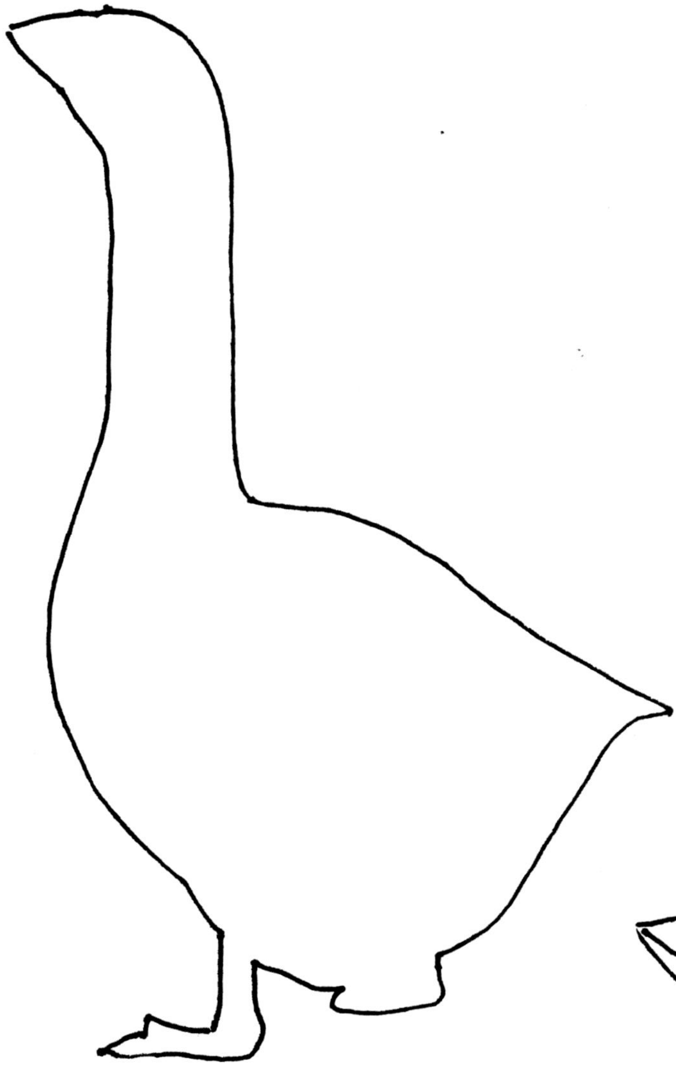

I recommend you use this pattern at full size. The wood thickness can be 1/8", 1/4", or 1/2".

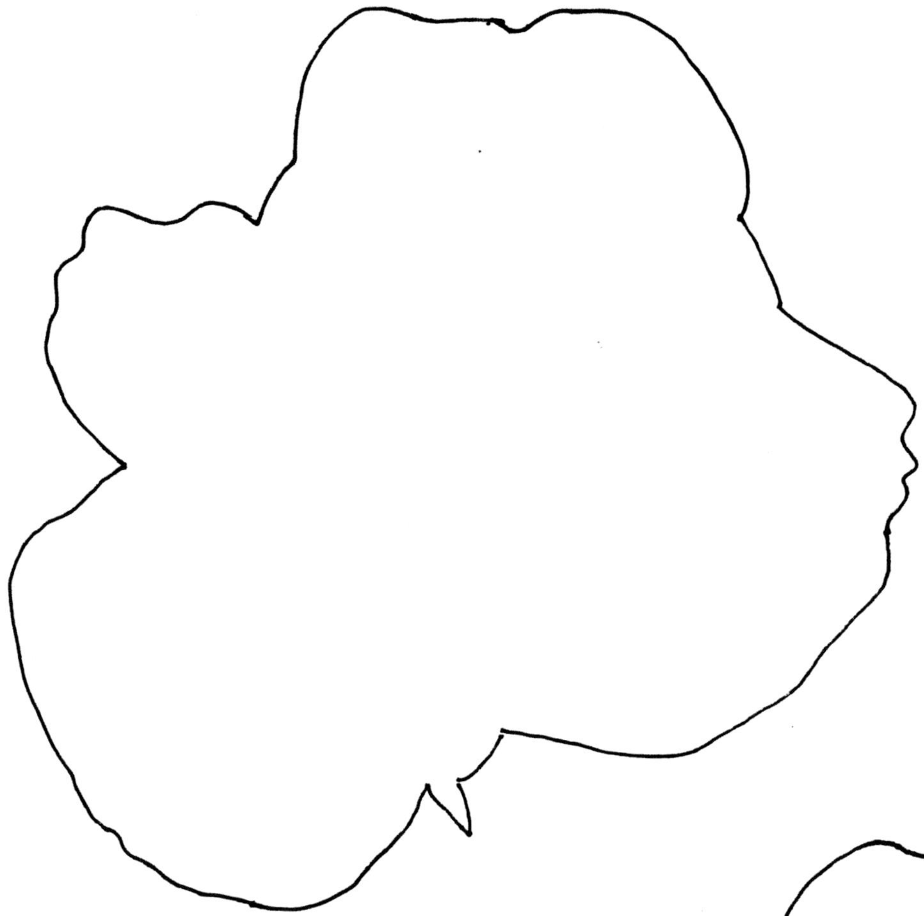

I recommend you use this pattern at full size. The wood thickness can be 1/8", 1/4", or 1/2".

I recommend you use this pattern
at full size. The wood thickness
can be 1/8", 1/4", or 1/2".

I recommend you use this pattern at full size. The wood thickness can be 1/8", 1/4", or 1/2".

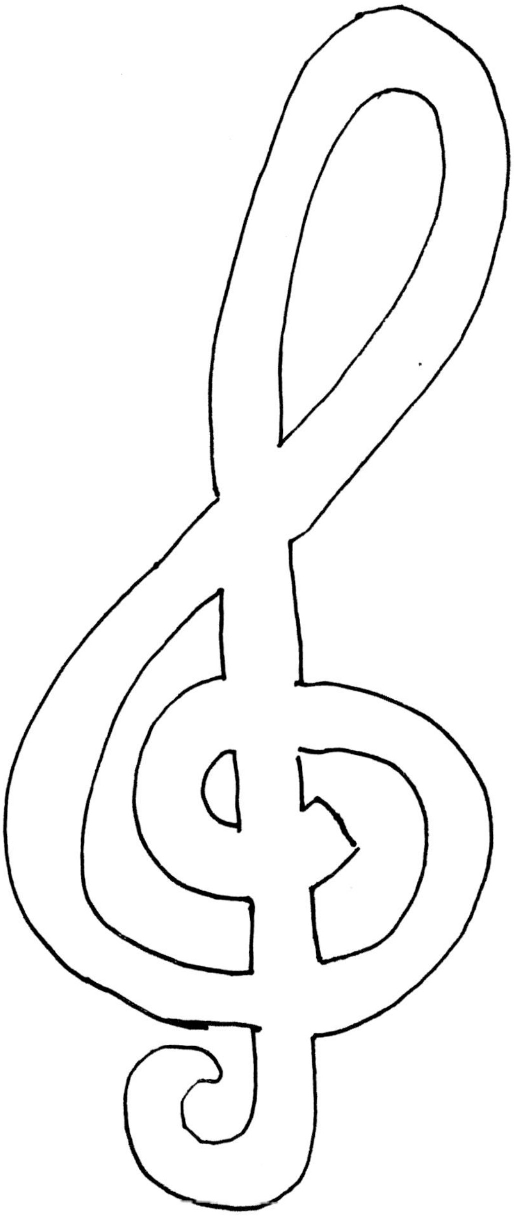

I recommend you use this pattern at full size. The wood thickness can be 1/8", 1/4", or 1/2".

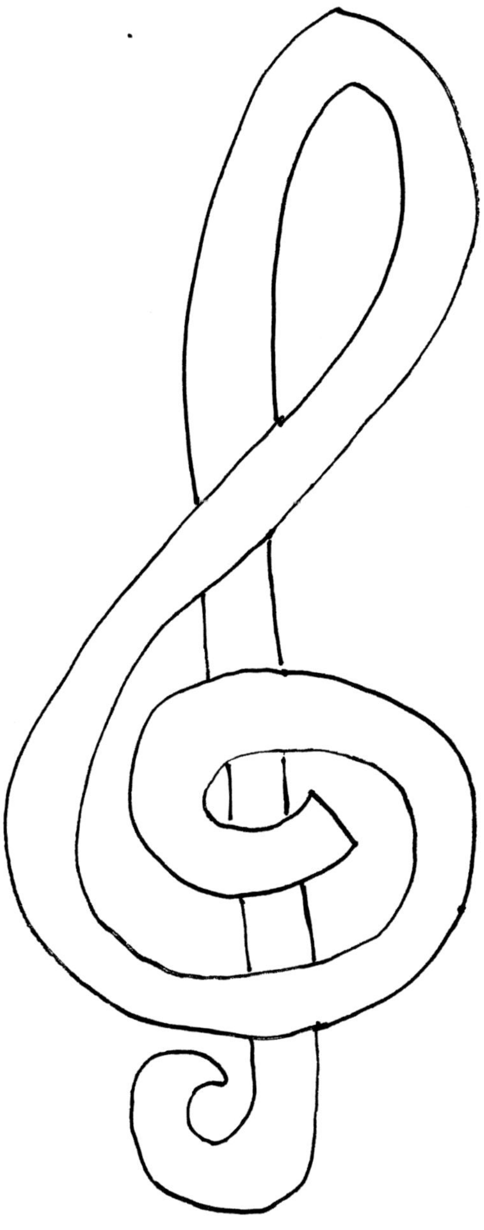

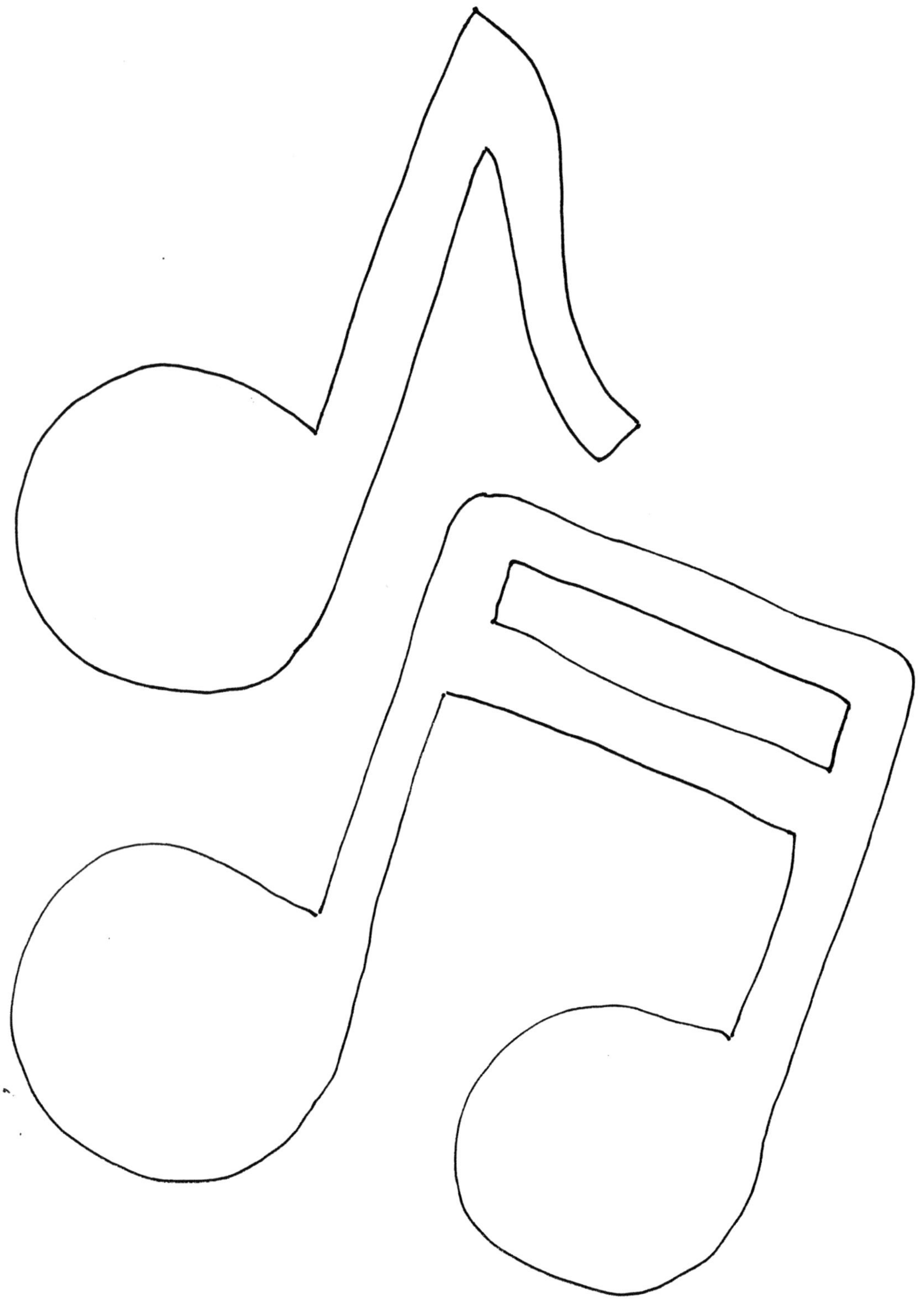

I recommend you use this pattern at full size. The wood thickness can be 1/8", 1/4", or 1/2".

I recommend you use this pattern at full size. The wood thickness can be 1/8", 1/4", or 1/2".

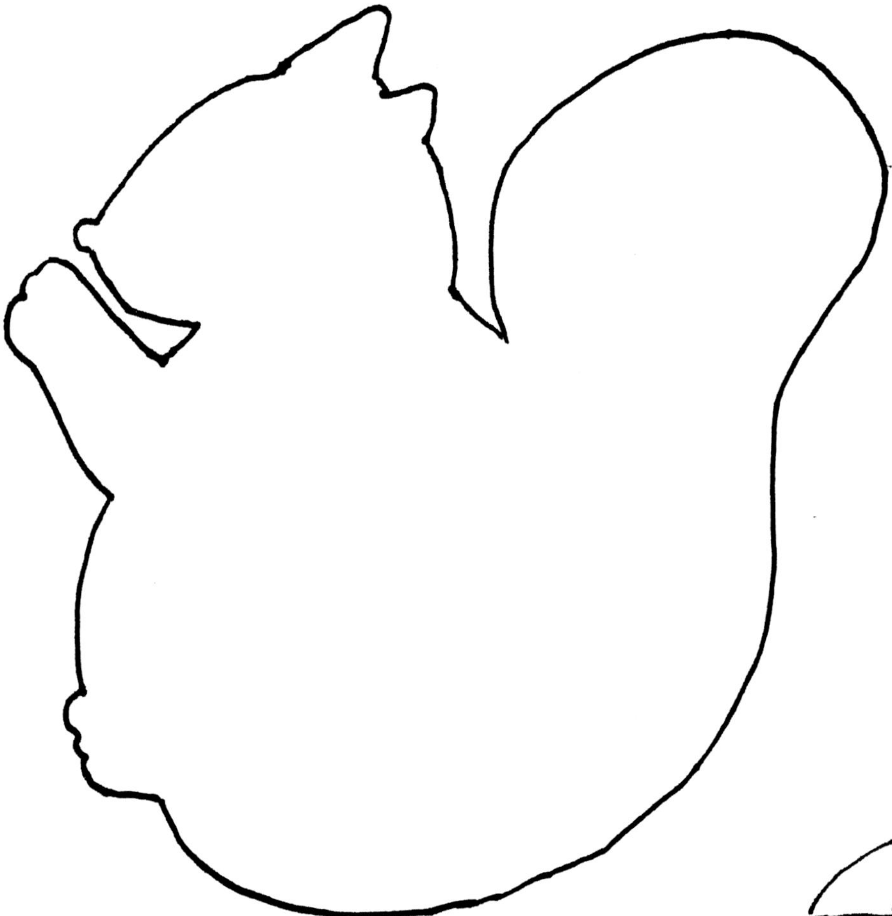

I recommend you use this pattern at full size. The wood thickness can be 1/8", 1/4", or 1/2".

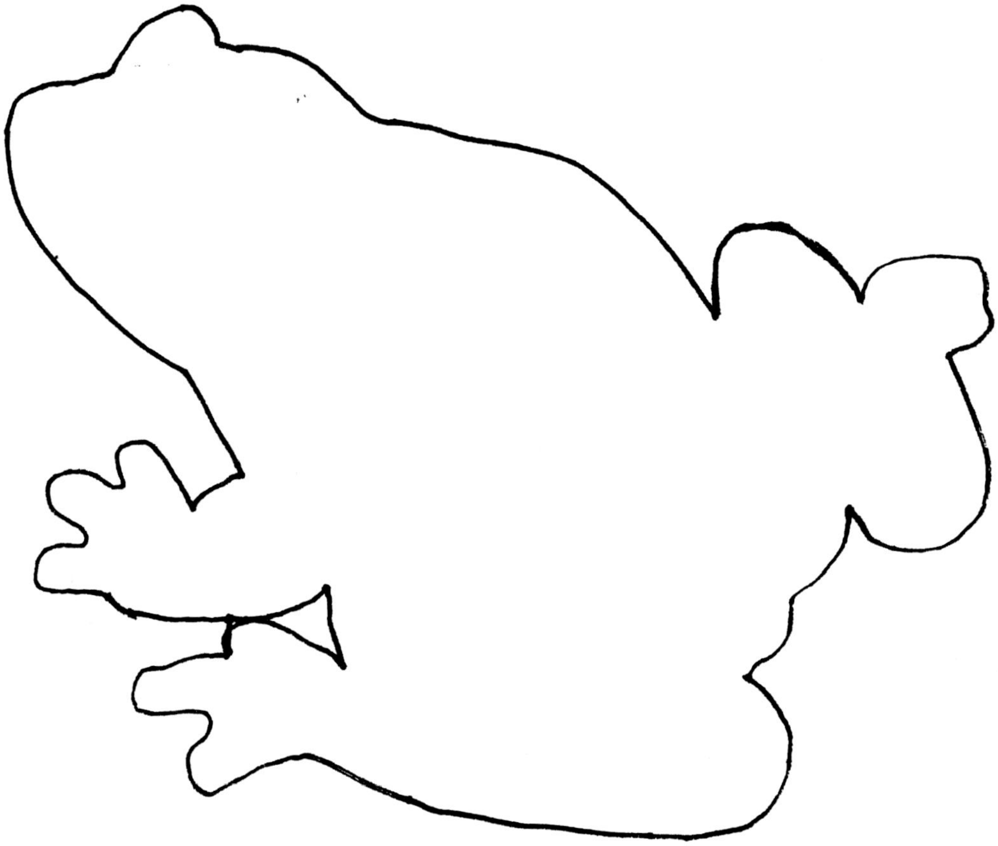

I recommend you use this pattern at full size. The wood thickness can be 1/8", 1/4", or 1/2".

I recommend you use this pattern at full size. The wood thickness can be 1/8", 1/4", or 1/2".

I recommend you use this pattern at full size. The wood thickness can be 1/8", 1/4", or 1/2".

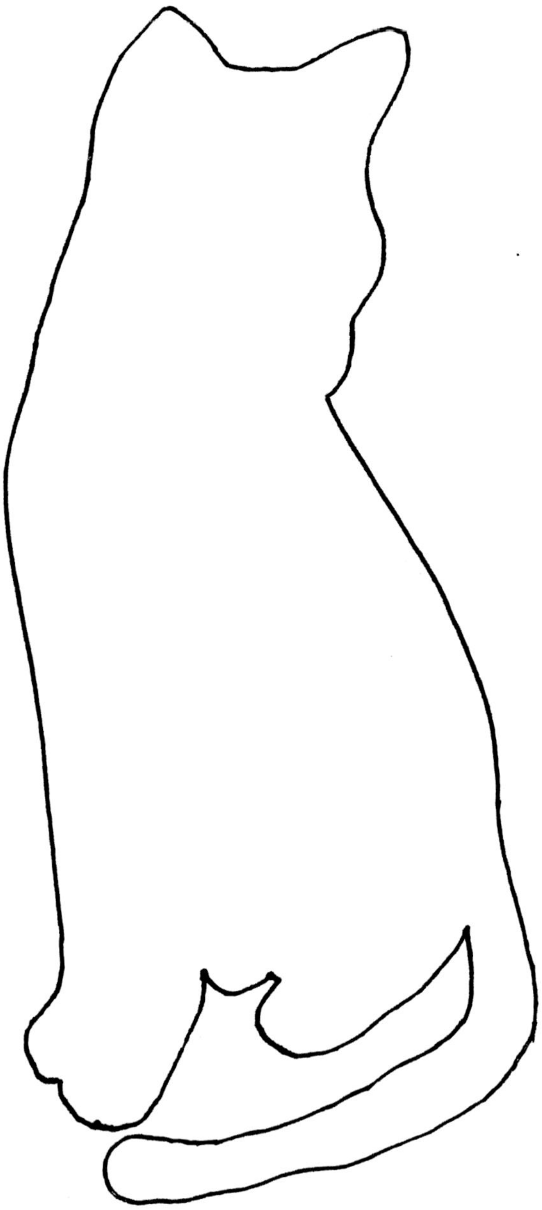

I recommend you use this pattern at full size. The wood thickness can be 1/8", 1/4", or 1/2".

I recommend you use this pattern at full size. The wood thickness can be 1/8", 1/4", or 1/2".

I recommend you use this pattern at full size. The wood thickness can be 1/8", 1/4", or 1/2".